IMAGINE LIVING HERE

THIS PLACE IS

WET

BY

VICKI COBB

ILLUSTRATED BY

BARBARA LAVALLEE

Walker and Company
New York

The author and artist gratefully acknowledge the support and assistance of the following: Eliane Freitas of the Brazilian Tourism Foundation; Scott A. Mori, curator, of the New York Botanical Gardens; Paolo Lavageto of Varig Brazilian Airlines; Ivano Freitas Cordiero, Claudia Simoes, and Huberto Cetraro of Emamtur in Manaus; Bruce Nelson and Francisco Colares of INPA; 2nd Sgt. Carlos Alberto Lima, Eury and Tralcy Barros, and Alionar Barros of Amazon Explorers; Dr. Francisco Ritta Bernardino of the Ariau Tower Lodge; and Ivandel Godhino of Embratur.

First published in the United States of America in 1989
by Walker Publishing Company, Inc.

Published simultaneously in Canada by Thomas Allen & Son
Canada, Limited, Markham, Ontario

Library of Congress Cataloging-in-Publication Data

Cobb, Vicki.
    This place is wet/by Vicki Cobb ; illustrated by Barbara
Lavallee.
        p. cm.—(Imagine living here)
    Summary: Focuses on the land, ecology, people, and animals of the Amazon rain forest in Brazil, presenting it as an example of a place where there is so much water that some houses need to be built on stilts.
    ISBN 0-8027-8880-6.—ISBN 0-8027-6881-4 (lib. bdg.)
    1. Rain forest ecology—Amazon River Region—Juvenile literature. 2. Rain forest ecology—Brazil—Juvenile literature.   3. Amazon River Region—Description and travel—Juvenile literature.
4. Brazil—Description and travel—Juvenile literature.   [1. Rain forest ecology—Amazon River Region.   2. Amazon River Region—Description and travel.   3. Brazil—Description and travel.]
I. Lavallee, Barbara, ill.   II. Title.   III. Series: Cobb, Vicki.
Imagine living here.
QH112.C63   1989
574.5′2642′09811—dc20   89-32445
                                                                          CIP
                                                                          AC

Printed in Hong Kong
1 3 5 7 9 10 8 6 4 2

The moment you step out of your airplane in Manaus, Brazil, you notice the humidity. Your skin quickly becomes coated with a thin film of moisture. Your clothes stick to you. You feel as if you have stepped inside a tropical hothouse. In fact, you *are* in a natural hothouse, an overgrown place called a tropical rain forest. The equatorial sun shines on puddles left by a recent shower that didn't cool things off. Air conditioning condenses moisture on windows, and carpeted rooms smell of mildew. The yearly rainfall here is about ninety-seven inches, more than eight feet, and the average humidity is eighty-five percent. No question about it; this place is wet!

Manaus is a city of a million people in the heart of the rain forest in northern Brazil, just south of the equator. It's on the banks of the Rio Negro, the "black river." The Rio Negro's water contains an acid from decayed plants that makes it the color of strong tea. It flows into the most enormous river in the world, the Amazon, which begins at a spring-fed lake high in the Andes Mountains of southern Peru. The river flows east across South America for 4,195 miles, where it empties into the Atlantic Ocean. The Amazon is not only the longest river in the world, fifty-one miles longer than the Nile, but it also contains the most water. More than a thousand streams and rivers join it on its way to the sea, forming a pattern like the veins on a leaf. Together, they contain more water than the next eight largest rivers combined. The land that they drain, the Amazon River basin, is about the size of the United States without Alaska or Hawaii.

The streams and rivers of the Amazon basin do not always stay in their banks. Flooding is normal six months out of the year. The high water mark in July can be forty to sixty feet higher than the low water mark in December. Forests and fields are flooded, islands and beaches disappear, and there are many new waterways among the trees. Houses on the waterfront float or are built on stilts. The Amazon near Manaus may be seven miles wide during the dry season, but during the wet season it is thirty-five miles wide.

Lots of water and warm weather are the best possible conditions for plant growth, and the rain forest is living proof. There are so many trees here that from the air the forest treetops look like an endless green cauliflower. A typical tree is 100 to 130 feet tall, with shallow roots, a thin bare trunk, and a small crown of leaves at the top. Its crown is right next to the crowns of other trees. The treetops form the roof of the forest which is called the "canopy layer."

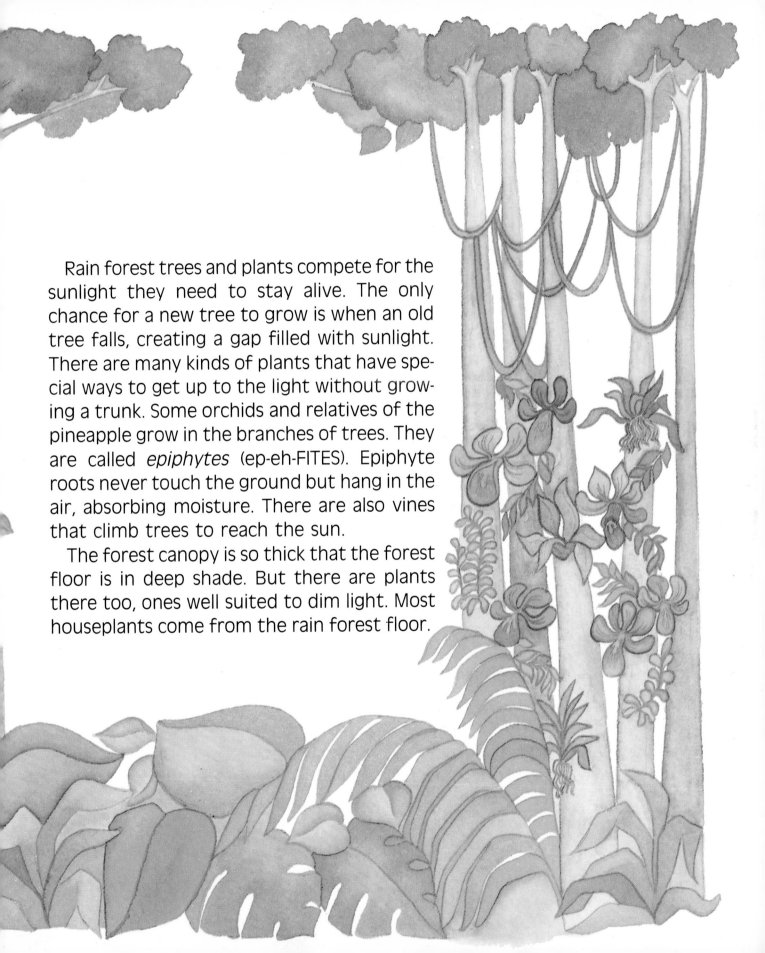

Rain forest trees and plants compete for the sunlight they need to stay alive. The only chance for a new tree to grow is when an old tree falls, creating a gap filled with sunlight. There are many kinds of plants that have special ways to get up to the light without growing a trunk. Some orchids and relatives of the pineapple grow in the branches of trees. They are called *epiphytes* (ep-eh-FITES). Epiphyte roots never touch the ground but hang in the air, absorbing moisture. There are also vines that climb trees to reach the sun.

The forest canopy is so thick that the forest floor is in deep shade. But there are plants there too, ones well suited to dim light. Most houseplants come from the rain forest floor.

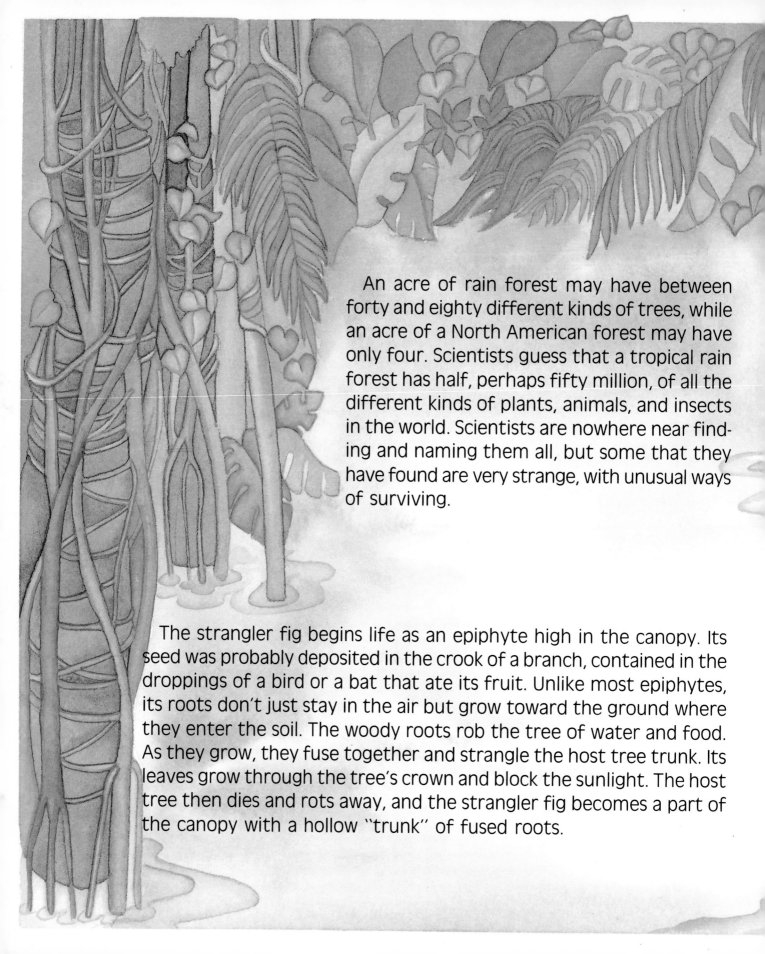

An acre of rain forest may have between forty and eighty different kinds of trees, while an acre of a North American forest may have only four. Scientists guess that a tropical rain forest has half, perhaps fifty million, of all the different kinds of plants, animals, and insects in the world. Scientists are nowhere near finding and naming them all, but some that they have found are very strange, with unusual ways of surviving.

The strangler fig begins life as an epiphyte high in the canopy. Its seed was probably deposited in the crook of a branch, contained in the droppings of a bird or a bat that ate its fruit. Unlike most epiphytes, its roots don't just stay in the air but grow toward the ground where they enter the soil. The woody roots rob the tree of water and food. As they grow, they fuse together and strangle the host tree trunk. Its leaves grow through the tree's crown and block the sunlight. The host tree then dies and rots away, and the strangler fig becomes a part of the canopy with a hollow "trunk" of fused roots.

The shallow roots of rain forest trees are not a good anchor in strong winds or floods. Vines and closeness to other trees help to keep them from blowing over. Some trees, like the giant kapok, have flat buttresses around the bottom of the trunk for added support. These buttresses make a booming sound, like a drum, when hit. Rain forest Indians communicate through the forest by striking them.

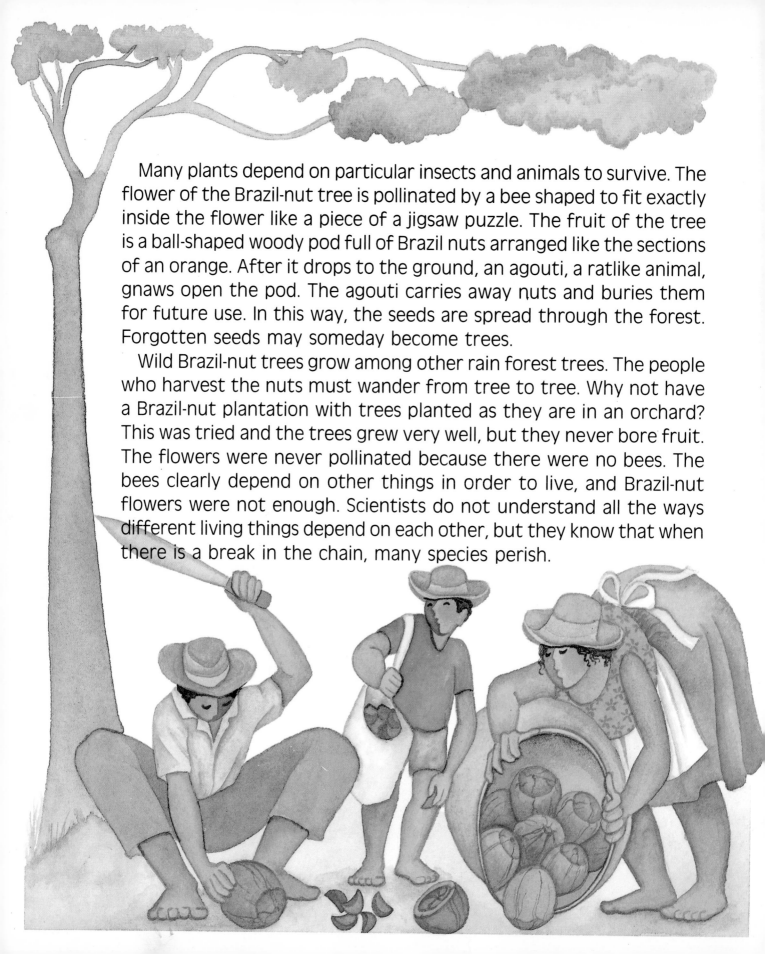

Many plants depend on particular insects and animals to survive. The flower of the Brazil-nut tree is pollinated by a bee shaped to fit exactly inside the flower like a piece of a jigsaw puzzle. The fruit of the tree is a ball-shaped woody pod full of Brazil nuts arranged like the sections of an orange. After it drops to the ground, an agouti, a ratlike animal, gnaws open the pod. The agouti carries away nuts and buries them for future use. In this way, the seeds are spread through the forest. Forgotten seeds may someday become trees.

Wild Brazil-nut trees grow among other rain forest trees. The people who harvest the nuts must wander from tree to tree. Why not have a Brazil-nut plantation with trees planted as they are in an orchard? This was tried and the trees grew very well, but they never bore fruit. The flowers were never pollinated because there were no bees. The bees clearly depend on other things in order to live, and Brazil-nut flowers were not enough. Scientists do not understand all the ways different living things depend on each other, but they know that when there is a break in the chain, many species perish.

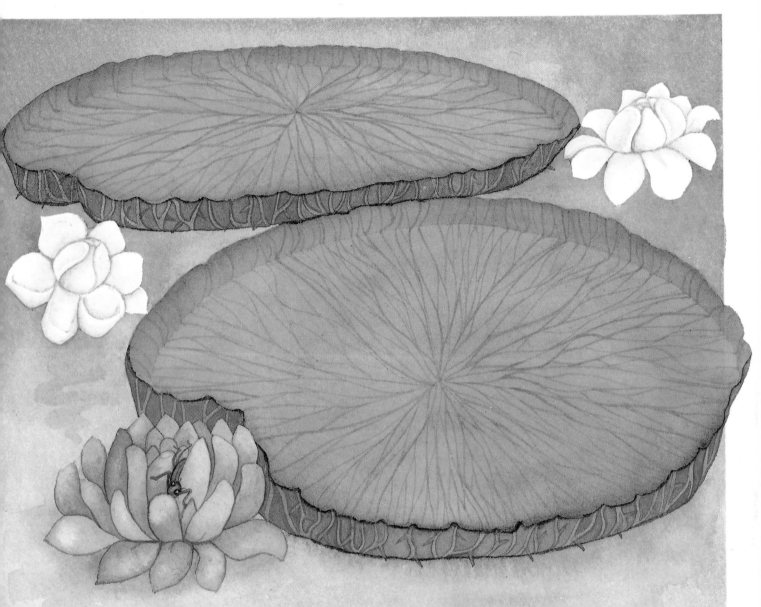

The lily pads of the Victoria royal water lily, which grow in shallow backwaters, can be eight feet across. Underneath, the heavy ribs of its leaf have spines to protect it from plant-eating fish. Its large white flower has a special relationship with the beetles that pollinate it. When it opens at sunset it smells like a ripe pineapple and is warm—as much as nine degrees warmer than the air. Immediately, large brown beetles begin to arrive. They feed in the center of the flower. A few hours later, the flower closes, trapping the beetles until the following evening when the flower opens again. But this time the flower is cool, no longer smells, and is a deep red or purple color. The beetles crawl out, covered with pollen, which they deliver to the next white flower they visit that evening. The beetle gets its meal, and the royal water lily gets pollinated.

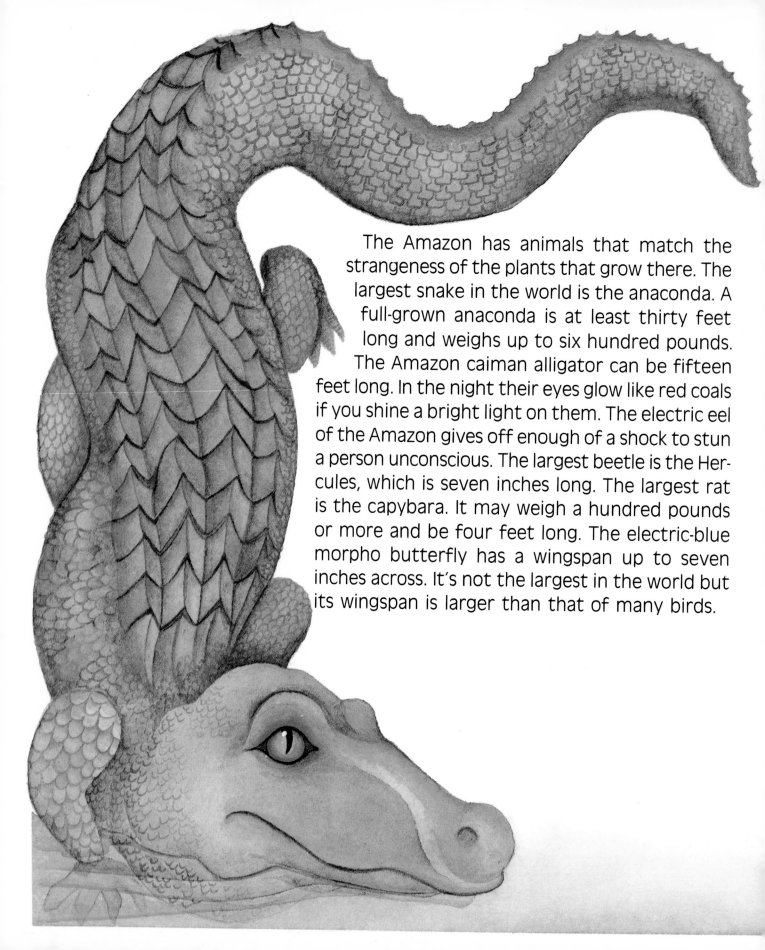

The Amazon has animals that match the strangeness of the plants that grow there. The largest snake in the world is the anaconda. A full-grown anaconda is at least thirty feet long and weighs up to six hundred pounds. The Amazon caiman alligator can be fifteen feet long. In the night their eyes glow like red coals if you shine a bright light on them. The electric eel of the Amazon gives off enough of a shock to stun a person unconscious. The largest beetle is the Hercules, which is seven inches long. The largest rat is the capybara. It may weigh a hundred pounds or more and be four feet long. The electric-blue morpho butterfly has a wingspan up to seven inches across. It's not the largest in the world but its wingspan is larger than that of many birds.

If you lived here you would eat a lot of fish from the Amazon River. One popular fish is called *tambaqui* (tam-bah-KEE) also known as the "fat fish." It can be three feet long and weigh sixty pounds. It has a mouth full of teeth perfect for cracking nuts and seeds. Its favorite food is rubber-tree seeds, which it turns into body fat. Broiled tambaqui tastes more like lamb than fish.

Tambaqui is a cousin of the fearsome, fifteen-inch piranha. Piranhas feed by taking bites out of other fish and animals with their razor sharp, triangular teeth. A school of piranhas has been known to devour a cow in a few minutes, each fish only taking a few bites. In spite of the many stories about ferocious piranhas, they don't often attack people. You *can* swim safely in certain parts of the Amazon.

Unfortunately, the Amazon river mammals have attracted hunters and trappers who have hunted them almost to extinction. The largest otter in the world lives here. This playful fishing champion can be more than six feet long. Its fur is particularly beautiful. Pink and gray freshwater dolphins leap out of the water at one of their favorite feeding areas: the meeting of the black water of the Rio Negro and the muddy waters of the Amazon. The two rivers flow side by side without mixing for about ten miles, until the muddy waters take over and give the Amazon the color of coffee with milk.

Manatees, or sea cows, graze on floating plants of the Amazon. They have been hunted for their meat and skin, which makes soft leather. All of the river mammals are now protected by law.

Some animals of the rain forest live up in the canopy and almost never touch the ground their whole lives. The slow-moving sloth spends its life upside down, hanging from trees with its hook-shaped claws. Its fur grows from its belly toward its back so rainwater can run off easily in its upside-down position. Microscopic green plants grow in its fur, giving the sloth a protective green color.

Monkeys are the forest acrobats. The spider monkey's tail is twice as long as its body. It is a fifth hand as it swings through the treetops. At sunrise and sunset, the loud roars of the howler monkeys sound like the thunder of an approaching storm. Howlers travel in bands of about twenty monkeys. They howl to let other bands of monkeys know where they are feeding so they will stay away.

Even louder than the howler monkeys are the parrots. Their hoarse squawks fill the air at the end of the day as they fly in pairs to nest for the night. Parrot beaks are nutcrackers, strong enough for Brazil nuts. At night, the forest canopy is also noisy with the sound of bat wings. Many different trees depend on bats for pollination. Their drab flowers have odors similar to sweat or meat to attract bats. There are also many fruit-eating bats that spread seeds in their droppings.

One of the most dangerous animals of the jungle is the jaguar, a large, beautiful jungle cat that can weigh up to 350 pounds. Like all cats, it is a hunter and meat eater. It kills when it needs to eat. A full-grown jaguar will eat one animal the size of a capybara a week. It can easily climb trees and will swim after an alligator. Some Indian tribes will not let a young man be called a warrior until he has killed a jaguar by himself with nothing but a wooden spear.

But jaguar hunting is not the only way young people prove that they are worthy grown-ups. Some Indians tribes fill a straw mitt with tiny, venomous fire ants. A twelve- or thirteen-year-old boy or girl puts a hand into the mitt and lets the stinging ants bite away. The elders judge how well they stand the pain. If they don't seem brave enough, they get another chance at the ordeal the next year. Fire ant bites sting painfully for about a half hour. But some people have a delayed reaction weeks later. This can be anything from a bad itch to a fever and occasionally even death.

In spite of all the dangers of the Brazilian rain forest, strangers from Europe and other parts of the world have settled here. Manaus became a Portuguese fort in 1669. The Portuguese wanted to defend this area against the Spanish, who were colonizing other parts of South America. For many years Manaus was a sleepy jungle town. The people who lived here were mainly native Indians, missionaries, soldiers, and slaves imported from Africa.

At the end of the nineteenth century, the invention of the rubber automobile tire changed Manaus. The rubber trees in the rainforest bleed a sticky white sap called *latex* when the trunk is cut. Latex can be collected in little cups. When enough has been collected it can be combined to form straw-colored balls of raw rubber. Rubber brought thousands of people to Manaus. Some people made fortunes and built the city into a showplace of fancy houses and theaters. People came from all over the world to live in this splendid city.

But the boom lasted only twenty-five years. Rubber-tree seeds were smuggled to plantations in Malaysia. It was easier to collect latex from neat rows of trees than from wild trees growing here and there in the jungle. People no longer needed expensive rubber from Brazil. Manaus again became a quiet city.

Some settlers became farmers. They needed to clear away the trees in order to create fields and pastures. Since there were no roads to drag chopped-down trees away to sawmills, the fallen trees were burned. This kind of land clearing is called "slash and burn." The main farm crop is manioc, a starchy root that can be made into a cake or a pancake. It can also be made into a dry yellowish sandy powder that is sprinkled on foods like salt. You may know it as tapioca, which thickens tapioca pudding.

People thought that clearing the rain forest would produce rich farmland for many different kinds of crops. They were wrong. Rain forest soil is poor. Rotting leaves from the trees form a natural fertilizer, but when the trees are cut down, this source of fertilizer is gone. The rains wash the minerals out of the bared soil. Crops may be grown for only a few years on cleared land. It is too expensive to add fertilizer and minerals after the soil gives out, so the land is abandoned. Small cleared areas can become a part of the forest again, but large cleared areas don't recover. Farmers move on and slash and burn new areas of the forest.

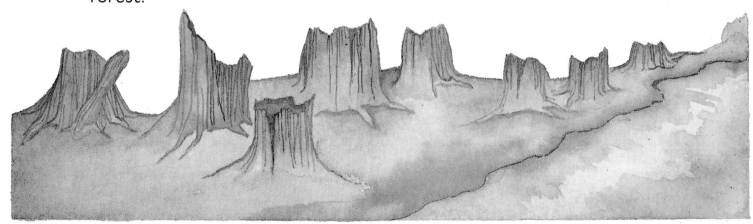

Today there is a monster machine that can clear a path in the rain forest four miles long and twenty-six feet wide in an hour. Its boom easily knocks over the trees, and knife-bladed rollers chop them up as it moves along. One of the largest government projects was the Trans-Amazon highway, which was bulldozed through the jungle in the early 1970s. The highway was supposed to open up the wilderness to new settlers, but it has been a huge failure. With the trees removed, there is nothing to hold the soil during the heavy rains. Unpaved roadways wash away. Soil washes away from under paved sections. Easy highway travel is impossible. A common sight along the highway during the rainy season is trucks stuck up to their hubcaps in the red mud.

The rain forest is also being destroyed for its valuable hardwood trees such as mahogany, and to get at gold, iron, and other riches in its earth. The Serra Pelada is a gold mine deep in the jungle. Gold was discovered here in 1980 when a tree was blown over and chunks of gold were found in the dirt around its roots.

The mine is run by the Brazilian government which lets miners work areas called claims. Each man gets a claim that is six feet by nine feet. There may be as many as 45,000 men working at one time. Since the men dig at different speeds, the claims are all different levels. After the earth has been sifted for gold, the dirt is carried out in bags, because there is no room for it in the mine.

People have to find a balance between the loss of the wilderness and the needs of the villages and cities.

The Balbina Dam is a hydroelectric plant near Manaus. It uses river water to make electricity. Since the Amazon doesn't flow fast enough to turn the turbines, the dam was built to create a huge lake. Water falling from the lake generates electricity, but the new lake flooded and destroyed thousands of acres of rain forest.

In the year it took for the new lake to fill, the rising waters trapped many animals. Two hundred and fifty men went out in canoes every day to rescue forest animals from drowning. No one knows how many were saved or how many more were lost.

The biggest destroyer of the rain forest is still man-made fires. On some days in the dry season, there are thousands of fires burning across the Amazon basin. Plants and animals that have not even been discovered are destroyed. More importantly, the fires are adding to the world's air pollution. One of the products of fire is carbon dioxide. Most of the extra carbon dioxide in the air comes from the burning of fuels in cars and factories. But burning the rain forest adds to the world-wide problem.

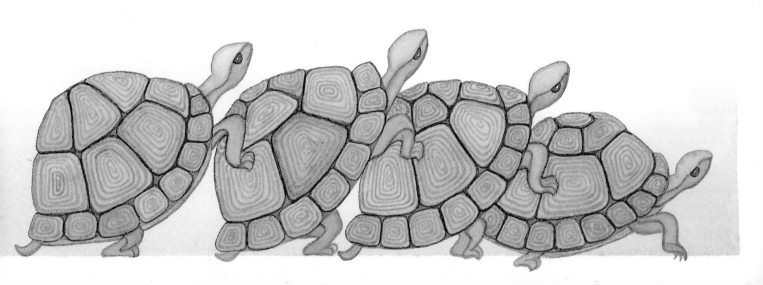

Carbon dioxide in the air traps heat coming from the earth's surface. A greenhouse does the same thing. In a greenhouse, the suns rays pass through the glass and warm up the soil and plants. The glass prevents the heat from escaping. Trapped heat makes the greenhouse get warmer. As carbon dioxide is added to the earth's atmosphere, it creates a *greenhouse effect*. The earth will get warmer. The ice at the poles could melt, raising the level of the oceans. Coastal land would be lost, and the world's rainfall pattern would change. No one knows for certain what will happen if the earth warms up. But if we wait to find out, it may be too late to do anything about it.

We do know that destroying the forest will change the climate of the rain forest. Less rain will fall. Here's why. Great amounts of water evaporate into the air over the Atlantic Ocean. Rainy weather travels west over the Amazon basin. The forest absorbs rainwater like a sponge. But the trees return more than half of this rainwater to the air. The same water comes down again as rain further west. If large areas of rain forest are destroyed, rainwater could not be recycled. Heavy rains would not be absorbed by trees, so there could be flooding. The minerals and plant foods would be washed out of the soil. The area could become a desert. Scientists don't know for certain that this will happen, but why wait and find out when it's too late to fix it?

The scattered native Indian tribes of the rain forest know how to live in harmony with the jungle. They know its foods and its poisons. They know its medicines, some of which have helped the rest of the world. They create art from its plants and animals. There is much we can learn from them.

There is also a great deal to learn from the rain forest. Scientists come here from all over the world to study the plants and animals and the ways they depend on each other.

Here we can learn the balance between civilization and the wilderness. People who live here use their imagination. They imagine ways to protect the jungle so they can keep on living here.